I0703404

Table of

CONTENTS

DEDICATION

To all the Drummond family chefs:

The vision I had for Putting It Down In The Kitchen came from seeing my late mother, Annelle Drummond, cooking in the kitchen. As I grew up, she had me and my sister Parama help her by doing things around the kitchen, like chopping up potatoes for her potato salad. I saw how my mother never measured her seasonings. She just sprinkled a little bit here and a little bit there, and her food tasted amazing.

My Grandma Drummond in Norfolk, Virginia cooked with commercial cooking pots that held large amounts of food, and she and my great-uncle Tinababy (yes, that was his name) cooked for the entire family. I was told that my great-uncle cooked at the naval shipyard. I saw measuring cups and spoons in the kitchen that they never used when they cooked. When I was a little girl, I saw how many people came to Grandma's house to get a plate of home cooking. These days, my brother, niece, and great-nephew are into cooking. It's good to see that this talent has passed down through three generations.

I remember my mother's sister, Connie Easterling, using leftover chicken and making her delicious homemade soup.

Aunt Connie, thank you for making this soup. I learned to master it, and I still make it today!

We're putting it down in the kitchen!

INTRODUCTION

Putting It Down In The Kitchen is an inspiring anthology that brings together ten talented home cooks from diverse backgrounds. Each contributor shares their love for cooking through a collection of recipes that have been cherished in their families and communities for generations.

Whether you're looking to recreate a beloved family dish or discover new flavors, this anthology serves as a testament to the joy and connection that cooking can bring into our lives.

Dr. Tenaria Drummond-Smith and co-authors invite you into their kitchens, offering a taste of their culinary heritage and a celebration of the meals that have nourished their loved ones.

STUFFED MINI SWEET PEPPERS & CHEESE

HOME CHEF
Germaine Miller-Summers

HOME CHEF
Dr. Tenaria Drummond-Smith

HOME CHEF
Dr. Tenaria Drummond-Smith
PUTTING
IT DOWN IN THE
KITCHEN

HOMEMADE RIB TIPS

HOME CHEF
Dr. Tenaria Drummond-Smith

DIRECTIONS

To clean your rib tips, first rinse them with cold water. Use a knife to remove any excess fat that might be on them. Also, remember to remove the membrane from the meat. Drain the rib tips and place them in a pot of water. Add a ½ capful of vinegar and meat tenderizer to the pot. Cover the pot and simmer on a low flame for about five minutes. While the rib tips are simmering, preheat your oven to 300°F.

Remove the rib tips and drain. Season them and put them into an aluminum foil pan. Cover the pan and cook them in the oven until they are tender and to your liking. Remove the pan cover and let the stove brown the rib tips.

After you brown the rib tips, they are ready to eat, but you can add BBQ sauce for sticky rib tips. It's your preference. Add BBQ sauce to your rib tips for sticky rib tips and put them back in the oven for about 5 to 10 minutes

INGREDIENTS

Vinegar

Onion powder

All-purpose seasoning

Seasoned meat tenderizer

Mrs. Dash Garlic and Herb seasoning blend

Sweet Baby Ray's barbecue sauce or any BBQ sauce of your choice

CHICKEN & SAUSAGE DIRTY RICE

HOME CHEF
Dr. Tenaria Drummond-Smith

INGREDIENTS

Drumsticks
Sage sausage
Olive oil
Rice
All purpose seasoning
Garlic powder
Pepper
Mrs. Dash Original seasoning blend

DIRECTIONS

How to cook the rice

I prefer drumsticks with my rice but, use any part of the chicken.

1. Clean the chicken thoroughly and cook with the skin on. After the chicken is cooked, add seasoning.
2. Chop one whole onion and add it to your cooking pot with olive oil and all seasonings. Slowly fry the onions and seasonings until they are brown and soft.
3. Add water to the pot, then add the chicken. Add additional seasonings to the pot before the water begins to boil.
4. Let the pot boil until the chicken starts falling off the bone. Remove the chicken from the broth and let it cool so you can shred it. Keep the broth because it will be added to the rice.
5. Cut up the sage sausage and fry until done. Add a little water to the frying pan to use all the oil from the sausage, which you will later add to the chicken broth.
6. Add your rice of choice, shredded chicken, and chopped sage sausage in a large pot. Mix everything up and add a little more seasoning if needed.
7. Add water and olive oil to the water in the pot. Then stir everything up before covering the pot.

DIRECTIONS

Split your collard greens one by one. You can remove the stems or leave them on. Fold two or three leaves together and cut them into smaller pieces. Once the greens are cut, put them in water and wash them with a teaspoon or two of baking soda to remove all the dirt. Rinse and repeat with clean water.

Add oil, stock, and seasonings to boiling water in your cooking pot. Next, add your greens to the water a bit at a time. When all the greens are in the pot, cover the pot until the greens start boiling. You can add additional seasoning to your liking.

Then, cook your greens on a low to medium flame until they are tender enough to eat.

NO-MEAT COLLARD GREENS

HOME CHEF
Dr. Tenaria Drummond-Smith

INGREDIENTS

Olive oil
Onion powder
Garlic powder
Black pepper
All-purpose seasoning
Mrs. Dash Original seasoning blend
½ capful of apple cider vinegar
4 lb. batch of fresh collard greens
Turkey stock or any meat broth of your preference

CHICKEN & SAUSAGE DUMPLINGS

HOME CHEF
Dr. Tenaria Drummond-Smith

DIRECTIONS

1 Wash the chicken breasts, cube them, and then add them to a pot of water with your dry seasonings. Boil the chicken until done.

2. Cut up the sage sausage, fry it until done, then add it to the cooked chicken.

3. Open the can of biscuits and cut each into four or six pieces (this will depend on how large you prefer your dough). Add them to the chicken and sausage mix and cook until done. Add more water if needed.

4. In another pot, add cream of chicken with the carrots and potatoes. You can add sweat peas and other vegetables if you like.

5. Set the pot on high heat. Once the pot starts boiling, reduce heat. Add the chicken and sausage mix and cook at a simmer. Season to taste.

INGREDIENTS

Chicken breasts
Carrots
Potatoes
Onion
Can of biscuit
Can of cream of chicken
Can or frozen sweet peas
Sage sausage
Garlic powder
Pepper
Salt
All purpose seasoning

DIRECTIONS

1. Preheat your oven to 350°F.

2. Mix the ground beef (or ground turkey) in a large bowl with the Italian sausage. Remove the skin from the sausage before mixing it with the ground beef.

3. Add all the seasonings (except parmesan cheese) to the meat. After mixing everything, let the mixture set for about five minutes and allow the breadcrumbs to soften before making the meatballs.

4. Roll meatballs into the size of your choice and put them on a baking sheet or aluminum pan. Bake for 15 to 20 minutes, or cook them to your preference.

5. In a separate sauce pot, add spaghetti sauce, sugar, garlic, sea salt, and onion powder. When the meatballs are cooked, drain the oil from the pan and add them to the sauce pot. Let the meatballs and sauce simmer. Plate your spaghetti with the sauce and meatballs and top with parmesan cheese.

HOMEMADE MEATBALLS

HOME CHEF
Dr. Tenaria Drummond-Smith

INGREDIENTS

Breadcrumbs

Garlic powder

Onion powder

Italian seasoning

Sea salt

Black pepper

Italian sausage

Ground beef or ground turkey

Eggs

Grated parmesan cheese

Sugar

HOME CHEF
GERMAINE MILLER-SUMMERS

HOME CHEF
GERMAINE MILLER-SUMMERS

SAUSAGE, EGG & CHEESE BREAKFAST MUFFIN

HOME CHEF
Germaine Miller-Summers

INGREDIENTS

1 can of Pillsbury Crescent Rolls
Large eggs and whole milk
Shredded cheddar cheese
Breakfast sausage (pork, turkey, or chicken)
Salt, pepper
Jalapeño peppers (chives or green onions will work too!)

DIRECTIONS

1. Mix the base: whisk eggs and milk together in a large bowl. Add salt and pepper to taste. Coat the bottom of a muffin tin with nonstick spray.
2. Build the cups: using the Pillsbury Crescent Roll, divide the perforated pieces into each muffin cup bottom and moisten sides. Divide the cooked, crumbled sausage among the cupcakes. Layer cheese on top.
3. Add the meat: ladle or pour the egg mixture over the sausage and shredded cheese. Add the jalapeño pepper on top in the center.
4. Assemble and bake: place in the oven on 350°F and cook for 18-20 minutes, or until the eggs are set and the tops are golden brown. Remove from oven and let rest for 5 minutes.

SWEET POTATO PANCAKES

HOME COOK CHEF
Germaine Miller-Summers

DIRECTIONS

Place mashed sweet potatoes in a large bowl. Add eggs, milk, brown sugar, and maple syrup.

Whisk until combined.

Sprinkle flour, cinnamon, baking powder, salt, and nutmeg on top of the sweet potato mixture.

Stir until smooth. Add melted butter and mix until combined.
.

INGREDIENTS

2 Backed or boiled mashed sweet potatoes
¾ cup all-purpose flour
2 large eggs
½ cup milk
2 tbsp melted butter
1 tbsp maple syrup
plus more for servicing
2 tbsp brown sugar
1 tsp baking powder
¼ tsp salt
1 tsp cinnamon
Pinch nutmeg

STUFFED MINI SWEET PEPPERS

HOME CHEF
Germaine Miller-Summers

DIRECTIONS

1. Start by preparing the filling, which includes soft goat cheese, grated parmesan cheese, garlic, black pepper, and fresh minced jalapeno peppers (removing the seeds and ribs cuts down on the heat significantly).
2. Combine the ingredients and stir into a fluffy, creamy filling.
3. Rinse a pound of mini sweet peppers, and slice them in half through the middle (you can cut the tops off if you prefer).
4. Place the cut peppers into a bowl with olive oil and salt. Toss until evenly coated.
5. Fill all the mini peppers with the prepared filling. There should be just enough to fill each pepper half generously.
6. Oven: roasting the mini peppers in the oven at 425°F for about 20-25 minutes.
7. The cheese should be slightly golden on top, and the peppers should be softened.

INGREDIENTS

**1 lb. mini sweet peppers
2 tbsp extra virgin olive oil
Salt
10-ounce log of softened goat cheese
2/3 cup of grated parmesan cheese (40g by weight)
1 tbsp minced garlic
2 jalapeño peppers, seeded and finely chopped (1/3 cup, measured)
¼ tsp freshly ground black pepper**

ARUGULA MIXED GREEN PIZZA

HOME CHEF
Germaine Miller-Summers

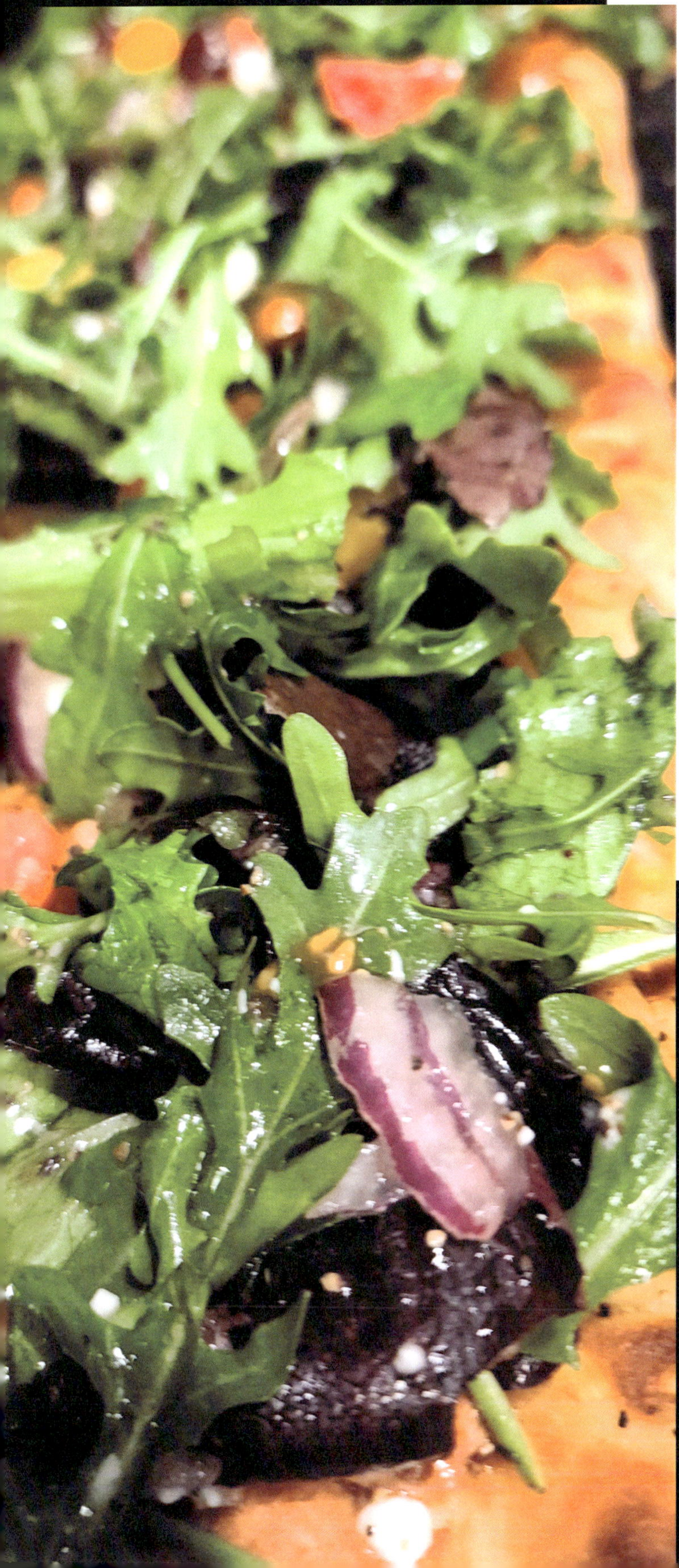

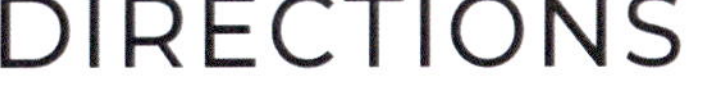

DIRECTIONS

Pizza crust:
1. Place ready-to-bake pizza crust on a cookie sheet.
2. Drizzle pizza crust with olive oil.
3. Slice or mince fresh garlic and spread it throughout the crust.
4. Sprinkle dried basil and Everything Italian Seasoning over the crust.
5. Spread shredded Mexican style cheese over the crust.
6. Bake in the oven at 350°F until the crust is toasted and the cheese is melted.

Salad:
1. Place arugula and mixed green salad into a bowl.
2. Slice the cherry tomatoes in half.
3. Add sliced red onion.
4. Add goat cheese.
5. Add bacon pieces.
6. Add salt and pepper.
7. Add lemon herb vinaigrette.
8. Mix everything together and spread over the pizza crust.

INGREDIENTS

Pizza crust:
Ready-to-bake pizza crust
Olive oil
Fresh garlic (sliced or minced)
Dried basil seasoning
Everything Italian Seasoning
Shredded Mexican style cheese

Salad:
Arugula and mixed green salad
Goat cheese
Cherry tomatoes
Red onion
Bacon strips (broken into pieces)
Salt and pepper
Lemon herb vinaigrette

SHRIMP & GRITS

HOME CHEF
Germaine Miller-Summers

DIRECTIONS

1. To make your shrimp stock, place shells in water and simmer until reduced by about half. Do this while the grits are cooking.
2. Make the grits: stir the grits into simmering chicken stock and cook. Stir until thickened. Add the cheese, sour cream, and butter and combine until thick and creamy. Turn heat off and cover while you prepare the shrimp.
3. Brown the sausage, remove and set aside. Crisp the bacon, render the fat, remove and set aside with the sausage. Cook the onions in bacon fat until translucent and starting to brown, then add the garlic.
4. Add the shrimp and seasonings and cook a few minutes until the shrimp is just about cooked through.
5. De-glaze the pan with the wine and shrimp stock, and simmer until reduced by about half.
6. Stir in the Worcestershire sauce and lemon juice.
7. Add the sausage and bacon back to the pan and combine to heat through. Swirl in a pat of butter, and add salt and pepper to taste. Spoon over grits. Sprinkle with parsley and serve immediately.

INGREDIENTS

Frozen extra-large shrimp peeled and deveined. (Tails reserved for the stock about 12-16)
4 pieces thick bacon strips
6 oz Andouille sausage, sliced into rounds
Onion, minced garlic, parsley
Cajun seasoning, smoked paprika
White wine
Fresh lemon juice
Worcestershire sauce, butter

Grits:
Quaker Grits follow instructions (or yellow or white cornmeal)
Parmesan cheese, sour cream, butter (to make them extra creamy)

HOME CHEF
Annette Mooring

HOME CHEF
Annette Mooring
PUTTING IT DOWN IN THE KITCHEN

PEPPER POT SOUP

HOME CHEF
Annette Mooring

INGREDIENTS

1/3 lb. salted beef
1 ½ beef chuck roast
½ bunch fresh chopped spinach
½ bunch fresh chopped collard greens
½ bunch fresh chopped kale
2 scallions
8 oz frozen okra
3 sprigs of fresh thyme
1 onion, chopped
2 carrots, sliced

2 bouillon beef cubes
2 tsp ground allspice
8 cups of water
1 can of coconut milk
1 scotch bonnet pepper, chopped
4 medium potatoes, peeled and cubed
½ lb. yucca, peeled and cubed
2 tsp cooking oil

DIRECTIONS

Add cooking oil to a 6 qt. pot on medium-high heat. Caramelize cubed salted beef and cubed beef chuck roast.

Add onion, garlic, and scallion. Let simmer for 5 minutes and stir occasionally.

Then add thyme, scotch bonnet pepper, ground allspice, potatoes, and yucca.

Stir in beef bouillon cubes until dissolved. Add water, frozen okra, and sliced carrots.

Lower heat to medium-low. Stir the pot occasionally. Add spinach, collard greens and kale.

Let simmer for 40 minutes or until the meat has reached the desired tenderness.

Stir in coconut milk and cook for another 15 minutes.

Remove from heat. garnish with chopped scallion and serve.

BLACKENED SALMON

HOME CHEF
Annette Mooring

DIRECTIONS

Rinse 2 lbs. salmon fillet and pat dry.
Brush both sides with melted butter.

In a small bowl combine salt, onion,
garlic, dried oregano, thyme, paprika,
ground black pepper, and cayenne
pepper.

Then, evenly coat the salmon fillets
with spice mixture.

Heat a large skillet on medium heat.
Add the salmon fillet, skin side up, to
the skillet and cook for 3-4 minutes.

Turn the salmon fillet over, cooking
on medium heat until skin becomes
crispy. Remove from pan and serve.

INGREDIENTS

SPICE RUB

2 tsp salt

1 tsp granulated onion

1 tsp granulated garlic

1 tsp dried oregano

2 tsp paprika

1 tsp dried thyme

2 tsp black pepper

½ tsp cayenne pepper

Rinse red snapper with lemon/lime juice and cold water, Pat skin dry and coat 2 lbs. red snapper with all-purpose seasoning, onion powder, garlic powder, black pepper.

In a skillet, heat vegetable oil on medium-high heat then add red snapper gently to the skillet. Pan fry until both sides are golden brown and crispy.

Remove from skillet and set aside. Julienne bell pepper and onion.

Mince garlic and scotch bonnet pepper, add to skillet on medium heat, and sauté for 2 minutes.

Place red snapper back into skillet, add cup of water, 1 tbsp browning, allspice, and dried thyme.

Simmer for 15-20 minutes. Garnish chopped scallion and serve.

BROWN STEWED FISH

HOME CHEF
Annette Mooring

INGREDIENTS

2 lbs. red snapper
Lemon or lime juice
1 cup of water
1 yellow onion
1 tbsp browning sauce
2 garlic cloves
1 bell pepper
1 tsp all-purpose seasoning
1 tsp onion powder
1 tbsp dried thyme
½ scotch bonnet pepper
1/3 cup of vegetable oil
1 tsp black pepper
1 tsp ground allspice
1 tsp salt

JERK MARINADE
HOME CHEF
Annette Mooring

DIRECTIONS

In a blender, combine salt, ground allspice, thyme, ginger, scallion, scotch bonnet, pepper, onion, garlic cloves, ground black pepper, ground nutmeg, low sodium soy sauce, and vegetable oil.

Blend to a coarse consistency.

In a large bowl, coat chicken with jerk marinade. Refrigerate overnight.

Grill chicken over medium heat turning occasionally until cooked through.

INGREDIENTS

2 tbsp salt

2 tbs ground allspice

5 springs of thyme

Fresh ginger

2 medium scallions

1 scotch bonnet pepper

1 medium onion, chopped

2 garlic cloves

1 tbsp ground black pepper

½ tsp ground nutmeg

½ cup of low sodium soy sauce

1 tbsp of vegetable oil

DIRECTIONS

In a blender, add raisins, pitted dried prunes, dried cherries, lemon zest, lime zest, orange zest, and red grape juice. Blend to a coarse consistency and set aside.

In a separate bowl: sift all-purpose flour, baking powder, ground nutmeg, and cinnamon, and set aside.

Then cream together sugar and butter until smooth, add vanilla extract, and continue to mix with an electric mixer at medium speed.

Add the flour mixture slowly. Add the blended dried fruit and continue to mix for 2 minutes.

Preheat oven to 350°F.

Cover the bottom of a 10-inch cake pan with parchment paper. Pour cake batter into a parchment-lined cake pan.

Bake for 45 to 50 minutes. Remove from oven, let cool for 1 hour, then enjoy!

BLACK CAKE

HOME CHEF
Annette Mooring

INGREDIENTS

½ cup of raisins

½ cup of dried cherries

½ cup of pitted dried prunes

1 tbs lemon zest

1 tbsp lime zest

1 tbsp orange zest

1 cup of red grape juice

1 cup + 1 tbsp all-purpose flour

4 tsp baking powder

1 tsp ground cinnamon

3 eggs

1 stick butter at room temperature

1 cup + 1 tbsp raw cane sugar

1 tsp vanilla extract

HOME CHEF
Catherine Myland

HOME CHEF
Catherine Myland
PUTTING
IT DOWN IN THE
KITCHEN

DIRECTIONS

Bring water to a boil, and season with a pinch of salt and a teaspoon of butter to taste. Rinse rice and add to boiling water. Cook for about 10 minutes or to your preference.

Rinse meat and season. Let marinate for about 30 minutes before cooking.

In a separate pot, add oil, curry, and garlic. Sauté for about 2 minutes or until dark. Pour in seasoned meat into curry and cook for about 20 minutes then add potatoes (optional).

(Optional) Fried plantain and sauté carrots: Slice a sweet yellow plantain. Add to a heated pan with oil. Let the plantain turn a nice golden color on each side. Remove from pan and set aside.

Cut a carrot lengthwise. Add to heated pan and sauté lightly in oil for 3 minutes.

RICE AND CURRY GOAT

HOME CHEF
Catherine Myland

INGREDIENTS

2 cups of water

1 cup of rice

2 lbs. goat, diced

1 lb white potato

2 tbsp curry

1 tbsp oil

2 garlic cloves

Seasoning: onions, seasoning peppers, garlic powder, and soul food powder seasoning

ESCOVITCH FISH

HOME CHEF
Catherine Myland

DIRECTIONS

1. Clean fish with lemon or lemon juice.
2. Add lemon to water and soak fish for 5 minutes. Remove fish and rinse.
3. Season fish with grated onion, garlic, and onion powder. Add pimento pepper.
4. Let sit in a pot for 2 hours (time limit is optional), then add heat the pot. Add oil as the pot begins to heat.
5. Let the fish turn a golden color on each side, then remove and let rest on a rack or paper towel.
6. Cut carrot lengthwise and add to onion and bell peppers. Add oil of choice to a separate pot. Saute the garlic in heated oil for 3 minutes, then add the other vegetables.
7. Add the vinegar and combine it with vegetables. Pour over fish in a bowl or tray.
8. Let stand for a few minutes before serving.

INGREDIENTS

2 lbs. fish (any kind)

500 ml oil

A pinch of salt (to taste)

1 lb of carrots

2 large onions

2 bell peppers

4 garlic pegs

1 lemon or 1 tbsp lemon juice

2 tbsp vinegar

Seasoning: onions, seasoning peppers, garlic powder, etc.

DIRECTIONS

Bring turkey neck to a boil and cook for 15 minutes. Then add one can of coconut milk and 2 cans of pigeon peas. Sauté seasoning separately, then add to the pot. Bring to a boil again. Then add 2 cups of rinsed rice. Mix the rice and peas, and add salt to taste. Bring to boil again, then reduce heat and cover until the water evaporates.

Oxtail:
Wash oxtail with lemon and vinegar. Season with onions, peppers, garlic powder, and soul food seasoning. Add 2 tsp of Grace browning to a heated pot. Add 2 tbsp of ketchup, then add oxtail. Cover and cook until tender. Add about ½ cup boiling water if needed.

STEWED OXTAIL WITH RICE AND PEAS

HOME CHEF
Catherine Myland

INGREDIENTS

1½ lb. turkey neck
2 lbs. oxtail
1 cups of rice
2 cans of pigeon peas
1 can of coconut milk
Pinch of salt to taste
2 tsp Grace Browning
2 tbsp Ketchup
Seasoning: onions, peppers, garlic powder, and soul food seasoning
Vegetables of your choice

RICE AND CURRY CHICKEN WITH VEGETABLES

HOME CHEF
Catherine Myland

INGREDIENTS

2 cups of water

1 cup of rice

2 lbs. chicken

2 tbsp curry

1 tbsp oil

2 garlic cloves

Vegetables: cauliflower, carrots, bell pepper, broccoli, etc.

Seasoning: onions, peppers, garlic powder, soul food seasoning

DIRECTIONS

1. Bring water to boil, season with pinch of salt and teaspoon of butter to taste.
2. Rinse rice, add to boiling water and cook for about 10 minutes (or to your desired taste).
3. Rinse meat, season with seasonings, and let marinate for about 30 minutes before cooking.
4. In a pot, add oil, curry and garlic. Sauté for about 2 minutes or until dark.
5. Add seasoned meat into curry and cook for about 20 minutes.
6. Rinse vegetables, add them to a saucepan, and steam with just a pinch of salt.
7. Serve at your desired taste.

DIRECTIONS

Bring turkey neck to boil and cook for 15 minutes. Add one can of coconut milk. Add 2 cans of pigeon peas and bring to a boil. Add 2 cups of washed rice. Stir to mix the rice with the peas and add salt to taste. Bring to boil again, then reduce heat and cover until the water evaporates.

Jerk chicken:
2 lbs chicken, washed and seasoned.

Chicken seasoning: combine 4 tablespoons of Walkers Wood jerk seasoning, a pinch of salt, a tablespoon of browning sauce, pimento peppers, all-purpose seasoning, fresh garlic, and fresh onion (optional: soul food seasoning). Let chicken marinate in the seasoning overnight.

Preheat oven to 350°F - 375°F on broil. Place chicken in a baking pan and cover with aluminum foil. Leave in the oven for an hour and 15 minutes.

JERK CHICKEN WITH RICE AND PEAS

HOME CHEF
Catherine Myland

INGREDIENTS

2 cups of water
2 cups of rice
2 can of pigeon peas
1 can of coconut milk
A pinch of salt to taste
½ lb. turkey neck
2 lbs. chicken legs
4 tbsp Walkers Wood jerk seasoning
1 tsp browning sauce

Seasoning: onions, peppers, garlic powder, fresh seasoning, 4 garlic cloves, pimento peppers, soul food seasoning (optional)

HOME CHEF
Dr. Lucina Clarke

HOME CHEF
Dr. Lucina Clarke
PUTTING
IT DOWN IN THE
KITCHEN

CRISPY CODFISH BALLS WITH SPICY MANGO CHUTNEY

HOME CHEF
Dr. Lucina Clarke

INGREDIENT

1 lb. salt cod
(boneless and skinless)
1 small hot pepper
1 onion
1 whole parsley
1 tsp of baking powder
1 cup of flour
1 cup of water
2 pimento peppers
2 garlic cloves
1 small sprig of thyme

MANGO CHUTNEY
1 mango
1 small hot pepper
3 garlic cloves
Cilantro
Salt
Sugar

DIRECTIONS

Soak salt fish in water overnight.

Drain and shred fish using a food processor.

Combine the dry ingredients, flour baking powder, minced garlic and sugar. Stir for about a minute then add onions, salted shredded fish, thyme, red bell pepper, scotch bonnet and parsley.

Whisk until ingredients have been blended. Then add water gradually starting from about 1/3 cup until desired thickness.
Heat oil to 350°F in a skillet or saucepan.

Carefully place spoonfuls of the batter into the hot oil and fry for 3 to 4 minutes, or until the fritters are crisp and golden brown. Remove from the pan with a slotted spoon and drain on paper towel to remove any excess oil.

MANGO CHUTNEY

Peel and cut mango in small pieces.
Put all ingredients in a food processor and blend.

LEMON BUTTER SALMON

HOME CHEF
Dr. Lucina Clarke

DIRECTIONS

1. Rinse salmon with lemon.
2. Pat dry the salmon.
3. Rub the salmon seasoning/dry rub on the salmon.
4. Let marinate for 10 minutes.
5. Heat a nonstick skillet.
6. Add butter.
7. Place salmon In a heated buttered skillet.
8. Sear for 3 minutes until brown on both sides.
9. In a small saucepan, mix lemon juice, butter, salt, and sugar and stir for 5 minutes.
10. Pour lemon butter sauce on seared salmon.
11. Let rest for 5 minutes.
12. Served with roasted potatoes and vegetables.

INGREDIENTS

Salmon
Salmon dry rub
Butter
Lemon
Pepper
Salt to taste
Sugar

DIRECTIONS

Rinse halibut with lemon, then pat dry.

Season with lemon pepper and garlic.

Heat a nonstick skillet. Add butter.

Place halibut into a heated skillet and sear on both sides until brown.

Halve the baby tomatoes and slice the onions.

Add the tomatoes and onions into the skillet. Let simmer for 10 minutes.

Serve with vegetables, rice, or pasta.

PAN SEARED HALIBUT WITH BABY TOMATOES AND ONIONS

HOME CHEF
Dr. Lucina Clarke

INGREDIENTS

Halibut
Butter
Baby tomatoes
Onions
Lemon
Garlic
Lemon pepper seasoning
A pinch of salt

SKILLET ROASTED CHICKEN AND VEGETABLES

HOME CHEF
Dr. Lucina Clarke

DIRECTIONS

1. Rinse chicken with lemon and pat dry.
2. Crush garlic.
3. Slice ginger.
4. Marinade chicken with garlic and ginger, salt and pepper to taste.
5. Heat skillet and add some oil.
6. Place marinaded chicken on heated skillet. Let brown on either side. Remove from skillet.
7. Slice onion, celery, and carrots. Put in heated skillet with the juices of the marinated chicken.
8. Cook for 3 minutes then place the chicken back on the vegetables.
9. Serve with rice or pasta or eat by itself. Enjoy!

INGREDIENTS

Chicken breast
Carrot
Onion
Celery
Garlic
Ginger
Salt to taste
Pepper
Vegetable oil
Lemon

CRISPY THAI CHILI ORANGE CHICKEN WINGS

HOME CHEF
Dr. Lucina Clarke

DIRECTIONS

1. In a large bowl, place chicken, dry rub, and salt. Toss together.
2. Heat a cast iron pan and add vegetable oil.
3. Pour the wet ingredients into the dry ingredients and stir until just combined (do not over-mix).
4. Coat the chicken in gluten flour. Shake off unwanted flour.
5. Check the temperature of the oil, then place coated chicken wings into the pan.
6. Cook wings until golden brown on both sides.
7. Toss with Thai orange sauce. Serve hot!

HOME CHEF
Sandra Whyte

HOME CHEF
Sandra Whyte
PUTTING
IT DOWN IN THE
KITCHEN

PORK CHOPS

HOME COOK CHEF
Sandra Whyte

DIRECTION

Season the pork chops with garlic, thyme, jerk seasoning, browning sauce, and grated ginger. Cover and let marinate overnight in the refrigerator.

In a saute pan, add coconut oil and allow it to heat up over medium heat.

Remove seasoned pork chops from the bowl and place into the saute pan. Cook until golden brown on sides.

Pour in ½ cup of water and let the pork chops cook until tender.

INGREDIENTS

3 pork chops, rinsed

1 medium onion, sliced

½ red bell pepper, chopped

1 tbsp of fresh thyme leaves

4 crushed garlic cloves

3 tbsp of Walkers Wood jerk seasoning

¼ tbsp of browning sauce

2 tbsp of Pickapeppa sauce (for the gravy)

2 tbsp of grated ginger

4 tbsp of coconut oil

ACKEE AND SALTFISH
AVOCADO ACKEE

HOME CHEF
Sandra Whyte

DIRECTIONS

Remove saltfish from water, rinse, and boil for 15 minutes. Drain, flake, and set aside.

In a large sauté pan, heat coconut oil over medium heat. Add sliced onion, garlic, scallion, and Scotch bonnet pepper. Sauté for 3 minutes.

Add flaked saltfish and black pepper. Stir for 2 minutes.

Gently add drained ackee and stir everything together. Be careful not to break up the ackee too much.

INGREDIENTS

1 can of ackee (remove from can, rinse in hot water, then drain and set aside)

¾ pound saltfish (soak in water overnight)

1 medium onion, sliced

1 stalk scallion, finely chopped

½ Scotch bonnet pepper, chopped

½ teaspoon black pepper

2 cloves garlic, crushed

4 tablespoons coconut oil

MINCED BEEF WITH VEGETABLES

HOME CHEF
Sandra Whyte

DIRECTIONS

In a sauté pan, heat the extra virgin olive oil over medium heat.

Add the ground beef, thyme, garlic, Lawry's seasoning salt,
and all-purpose seasoning.

Stir and cook until the beef turns golden brown.

INGREDIENTS

1 lb. of pumpkin, diced into small pieces
1 medium white onion, diced
1 ear of green corn, cut into 3 or 4 pieces
4 crushed garlic cloves
5 sprigs of thyme
2 tbsp of Kerrygold butter
2 scallion stalks, finely chopped
1½ lbs. of chicken, rinsed and chopped into small pieces
2 large Irish potatoes, cut into small chunks
½ lb. of carrots, sliced
2 celery stalks, chopped
1 rosemary sprig
½ cup of cooked butter beans
½ tbsp of salt
1 pack of Jamaican chicken noodle soup mix

PUMPKIN SOUP

HOME CHEF
Sandra Whyte

DIRECTIONS

In a medium pot, pour 1 ½ quarts of water and bring to a boil. Add the chicken, corn, and ½ tablespoon of salt. Let boil for 20 minutes.

Add Irish potatoes and pumpkin. Cook for another 30 minutes.

Add the butter beans, chicken noodle soup mix, and all remaining ingredients. Season to taste while allowing the soup to cook for an additional 15 minutes.

Serve and enjoy!

CURRY CHICKEN WITH RICE

HOME CHEF
Sandra Whyte

DIRECTIONS

In a sautépan, heat the extra virgin olive oil over medium heat.

Add the ground beef, thyme, garlic, Lawry's seasoning salt, and all-purpose seasoning. Stir and cook until the beef turns golden brown.

Reduce the heat to low, then add the bell peppers and onions. Stir for 5 minutes.

Add the steamed mixed vegetables and stir again.

Cover the pan with a lid, turn off the stove, and let it sit for a few minutes before serving.

INGREDIENTS

Chicken
Lawry's seasoning salt
Walkers Wood jerk seasoning
Crushed pimento
Jamaican-style hot curry
Paprika
Green onion
Green pepper
Garlic
Cilantro
Turmeric powder
Betapac curry powder
Chief Amchar Massala
Long grain white rice

HOME CHEF
Donna Owens Collins

HOME CHEF
Donna Owens Collins
PUTTING
IT DOWN IN THE
KITCHEN

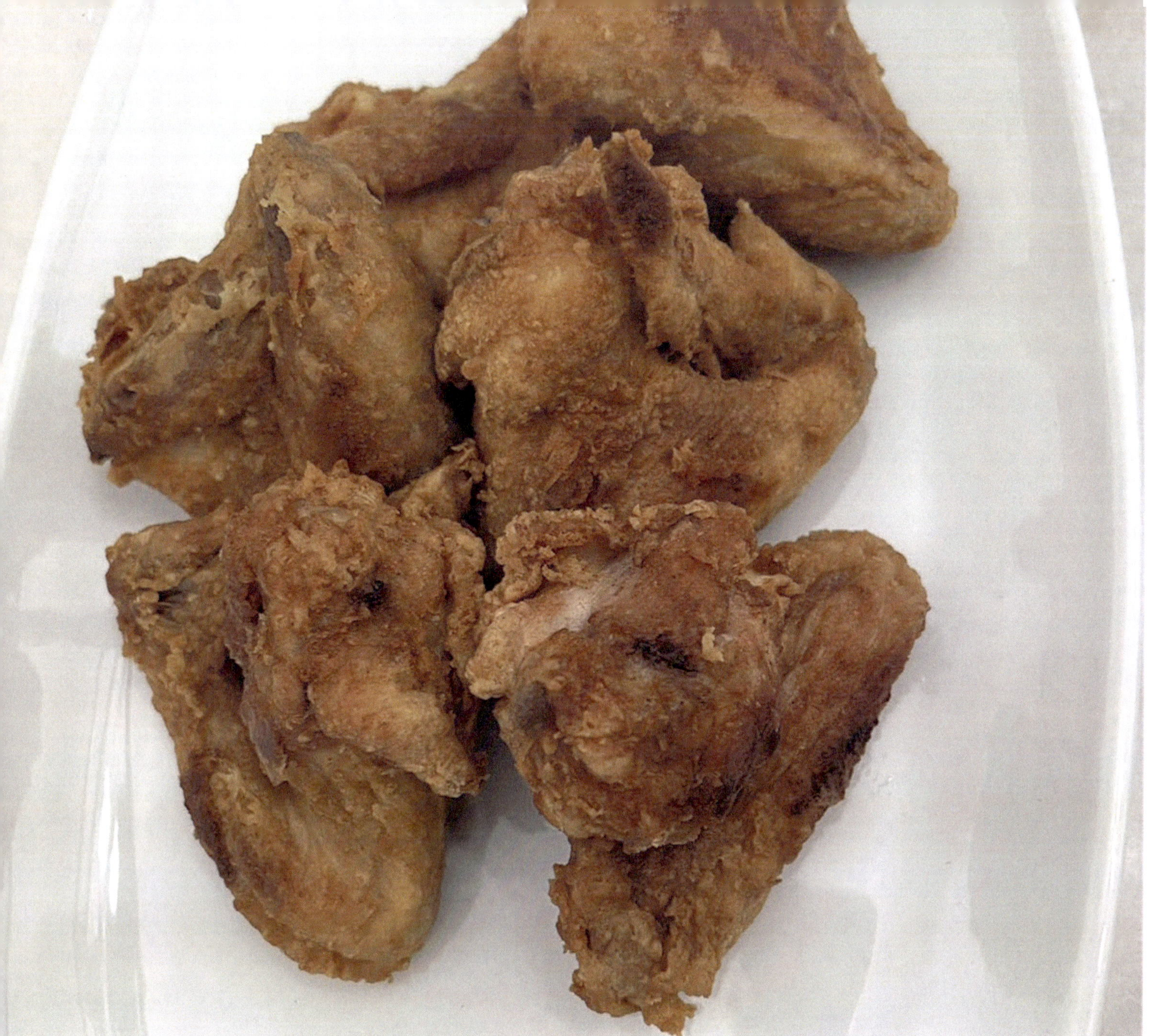

CRISPY CHICKEN

HOME CHEF
Donna Owens Collins

DIRECTIONS

Clean and season chicken to taste, using your preferred season salt.

After preheating, add oil to a large frying pan.

Flour wings and place into hot oil.

Turn them every 10-15 minutes until golden brown.

COW PEAS

HOME CHEF
Donna Owens Collins

DIRECTIONS

Soak beans in a bowl of warm water until swollen.

Boil smoked turkey or meat of your choice and season to taste.

After the meat is tender, add the beans to the pot and cook on medium heat (make sure that the water does not run out!)

Once cooked serve over rice.

INGREDIENTS

Cow peas

Smoked turkey or meat of choice

Salt

Pepper

Rice (optional)

STEW CHICKEN

HOME CHEF
Donna Owens Collins

DIRECTIONS

Season chicken and let marinate in refrigerator for an hour or overnight.

Brown chicken in a saucepan, then add a little water and let simmer in the browning sauce.

Once chicken becomes tender, add carrots and beans.

INGREDIENTS

Skinless Chicken

Onion

Garlic

Sazón

Mild jerk sauce

Carrots

White lima beans

CHICKEN WREATH

HOME CHEF
Donna Owens Collins

DIRECTIONS

Using a micro-cooker, shred steamed chicken, then broccoli, and add into a large bowl.

Add chopped onions, shredded cheese, chopped red pepper, and season to taste.

Add mayonnaise and blend everything together.

Layout the crescent roll into a ring. Once the ring is formed, spoon the chicken mix onto the roll and cover the mixture.

Brush the top with egg white. Cook at 350°F until golden brown.

INGREDIENTS

Boneless chicken breast
1 whole red pepper
Fresh broccoli
American cheese
Crescent rolls
Onion
Seasonings
½ cup of mayonnaise
1 egg white

POTATO SALAD

HOME CHEF
Donna Owens Collins

DIRECTIONS

Dice potatoes and add into a pot of water with eggs.

Cook the potatoes until firm, then drain water and let it cool.

Once cooked add in diced onions, eggs, relish, mayonnaise, a little mustard, and season to taste.

INGREDIENTS

5 lbs. of potatoes
Onion
Eggs
Relish
Mayonnaise
Mustard

HOME CHEF
Shamika Drummond

HOME CHEF
Shamika Drummond
PUTTING
IT DOWN IN THE
KITCHEN

MOROCCAN STEW

HOME CHEF
Shamika Drummond

DIRECTIONS

Preheat the pan with olive oil, tagine seasoning.

Add chopped onions, garlic potatoes, carrots, chickpeas, diced butternut squash, diced eggplant, tomato, bell pepper, and cauliflower.

Let simmer for 30 to 40 minutes.

Garnish with chopped parsley.

INGREDIENTS

2 tbsp. of olive oil
3 garlic cloves, finely chopped
4 shallots, finely chopped
5 cups of tomatoes, peeled and diced
3 tsp of Baharat spice
½ tsp of sweet paprika
¼ - ½ tsp. of cayenne pepper or hot chili powder (adjust to taste)
¾ tsp of salt (adjust to taste)
2 tsp of brown sugar
Black pepper, to taste
1 tbsp of tomato paste
2 cups of cooked chickpeas
1 medium sweet potatoes, cubed
2 tbsp of dried barberries or black currants
10 pitted black Kalamata olives

CAJUN CHICKEN

HOME CHEF
Shamika Drummond

DIRECTIONS

Marinate the chicken in the dry rub for 10 minutes.

Dry rub: Garlic powder, cayenne pepper, salt, pepper, onion powder, oregano, thyme, and olive oil.

Bake in oven at 350 degrees for 30 minutes.

INGREDIENTS

8 to 10 pounds of chicken breast
Garlic powder
Cayenne pepper
Salt
Pepper
Onion powder
Oregano
Thyme
Olive Oil

CAJUN SHRIMP DEVILED EGGS

HOME CHEF
Shamika Drummond

INGREDIENTS

2 dozen medium sized fresh shrimp
1 dozen eggs
1 tsp of cooking oil
½ small lemon
2 – 3 tbsp of mayonnaise
½ - 1 tbsp hot sauce (adjust to desired spice level)
1 tbsp of sweet relish
1 – 2 tsp Old Bay seasoning (+2 tsp for Cajun shrimp)
¼ tsp of garlic powder
2 tbsp of fresh chopped dill (+2 tsp for garnish)
Salt (to taste)
Pepper (to taste)

DIRECTIONS

Perfect Boiled Eggs
Gently place eggs in a shallow pot.

Fill with water, covering eggs. Once eggs begin to boil, turn heat off and cover for 15 to 20 minutes.

Cajun Egg Filling
Peel eggs, slice in half, and remove egg yolks to a medium sized bowl,

Place halved egg whites on paper towels to dry.

Starting with mayonnaise, add listed ingredients to the egg yolks and mix. Taste after each ingredient is added, and adjust to your liking and spice level. Mix until creamy, cover, and set aside.

Cajun Shrimp
In medium sized pan on medium/high heat. add shrimp and olive oil. Pat shrimp dry with a paper towel.

Add Ole Bay and stir until well coated. Saute shrimp until done (if raw) or until slightly charred.

Halfway through cooking, add about 1 tsp of lemon juice to shrimp.

Plating Cajun Shrimp Deviled Eggs
Garnish with paprika and dill.

HONEY GLAZED CHICKEN WINGS

HOME CHEF
Shamika Drummond

DIRECTIONS

Rinse chicken wings and set them aside. Mix all other ingredients in a bowl, then add the chicken wings. Once the wings are covered, place them on an oven pan and bake at 350°F for 40 minutes.

INSTRUCTIONS

Chicken wings

Honey

Paprika

Pineapple juice

Salt

Pepper

Cumin

BACON MACARONI & CHEESE

HOME CHEF
Shamika Drummond

DIRECTIONS

Place bacon in a large pan over medium high heat. Cook until crispy, about 4-5 minutes.

Add flour, then whisk until combined for about 30 seconds.

Pour in water and whisk until smooth and just thickened.
Add milk and whisk until combined.

Stir in pasta, salt. garlic powder, onion powder, smoked paprika, and pepper. Bring mixture to a simmer.

Cook for 10-12 minutes, stirring occasionally until pasta is done.

Turn heat to low, then stir in mild cheddar cheese, Colby jack cheese, sharp cheese, Romano cheese (Italian blend), and Bello Vitano cheese.

Keep stirring until sauce is smooth. Add heavy whipping cream, one tbsp at a time until desired consistency is reached. If you need to thin the sauce, add a little milk.

Stir in half the bacon. Sprinkle the remaining bacon over the top.

Place in the oven at 350°F for 15-20 minutes and top with extra bacon, if desired.

INSTRUCTIONS

½ box of elbow macaroni
1 cup of milk
½ cup of heavy whipping cream
10 bacon strips
2 tbsp of flour
1 pack of mild cheddar cheese
1 pack of sharp cheddar cheese
1 pack of Colby Jack cheese
1 small block of BellaVitano cheese, cubed
½ pack of Italian cheese blend (Romano and Parmesan)
1 tbsp of salt (to taste)
1 tbsp of garlic powder (to taste)
1 tbsp of onion powder (to taste)
1 tbsp of smoked paprika (to taste)
1 tbsp of black pepper (to taste)

HOME CHEF
Diane M. Stephens

HOME CHEF
Diane M. Stephens

DIRECTIONS

Bake a pan of homemade cornbread, using cornmeal as instructed.

Clean and boil chicken backs.

Cut onions, celery, and scallions. Add all ingredients into a boiling chicken pot.

Cook and remove from heat. After cooling, remove bones from the mixture.

In a large bowl, add baked cornbread and Stove Top stuffing. Pour chicken mixture into a mixing bowl with cornbread, broth, eggs, cream of chicken, and mushrooms. Mix well.

Bake in a preheated oven at 350°F until done, for approximately one hour.

Take the remaining homemade dressing and shape into muffins. Place them in muffin pan and bake for 15-20 minutes. Serve and enjoy!

STUFFING MUFFINS

HOME CHEF
Diane M. Stephens

INGREDIENTS

Stove Top stuffing mix

Chicken backs

Chicken broth

1 can of cream of chicken

1 can of sliced mushrooms

Homemade cornbread

Onions

Celery

Scallion

Eggs

SWEET CANDIED YAMS

HOME CHEF
Diane M. Stephens

DIRECTIONS

Cut potatoes into cubes or circles.

Add rinsed potatoes to a saucer pan with boiling water.

Add white sugar and brown sugar with butter.

Let cook at a medium temperature until the water boils out.

Sweet candied yams are done!

INGREDIENTS

Sweet potatoes

White granulated sugar

Brown sugar

Butter

Cinnamon (optional)

BROCCOLI CASSEROLE

HOME CHEF
Diane M. Stephens

DIRECTIONS

Mix crumbled crackers with Stove Top mix, cheese, can of cream of broccoli, eggs, milk, butter, salt, and pepper.

Mix well, adding broccoli and seasoning salt, (optional).

Pour in a baking dish and bake at 350 degrees for approximately 40 minutes until done and golden brown.

INGREDIENTS

1 bunch of broccoli
Ritz crackers
1 can of cream of broccoli
Stove Top stuffing mix
Sharp cheddar cheese
Milk
Eggs
Salt
Pepper
Seasoning salt (optional)

POTATO SALAD

HOME CHEF
Diane M. Stephens

DIRECTIONS

1. Boil potatoes and eggs until done. Peel eggs and chop into small pieces or mash.
2. Add mayonnaise and mix together with sweet relish.
3. Add small portions of mustard for color, and sprinkle top with paprika.

INGREDIENTS

Potatoes
Eggs
Mayonnaise
Sweet relish
Mustard
Paprika

GERMAN CHOCOLATE CAKE

HOME CHEF
Diane M. Stephens

INGREDIENTS

Box of devil's food cake mix

1 box of instant pudding mix

1 container of Cool Whip

1 pack of walnuts

1 pack of coconut

DIRECTIONS

Prepare and bake the cake as per instructions. Let cool and cut it in half.

Make pudding as per instructions and let cool in the refrigerator.

Fold in a container of Cool Whip.

Place walnuts and coconut together in a saucer pan, and brown in the oven or on the stove top.

Cover bottom layer of cake with pudding mixture, and sprinkle with coconut and walnut mixture.

Place remaining layer of cake on top of the bottom layer.

Repeat with the pudding layer, and sprinkle with the coconut and walnut mixture.

HOME CHEF
Dr. Carolyn Tabb

HOME CHEF
Dr. Carolyn Tabb
PUTTING
IT DOWN IN THE
KITCHEN

ORANGE MARMALADE BAKED MARINATED LAMB CHOPS

HOME CHEF
Dr. Carolyn Tabb

INGREDIENTS

4 lamb chops

FOR THE MARINADE:
1 cup orange marmalade
¼ cup pineapple juice
¼ cup brown sugar
¼ cup Yellow French's mustard
1 tsp sea salt
1 tsp black pepper
¼ tsp minced garlic

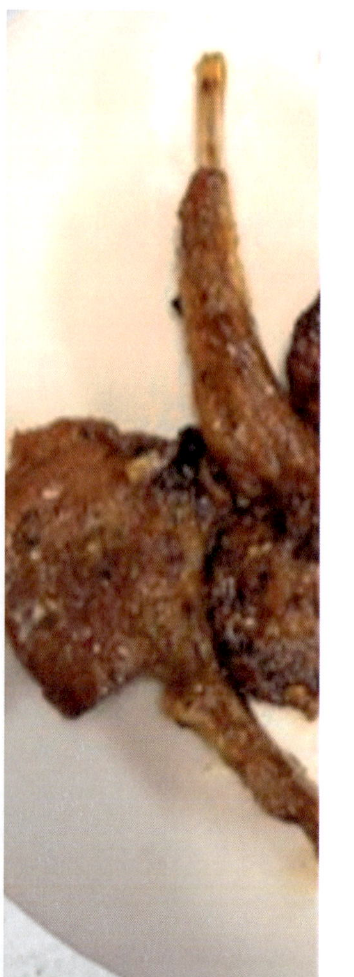

DIRECTIONS

MARINADE: Mix ingredients and turn to coat in a zip lock bag or mixing bowl. Marinate for at least 1 hour or overnight for up to 24 hours. Longer than the recommended time can cause the meat to become mushy.

SEAR: Heat olive oil in a large cast iron pan unit hot, Add lamb chops in a single layer and sear until browned. Flip and sear the other side.

BAKE: Immediately transfer the skillet to your oven, and roast lamb chops in the oven to the desired doneness. After lamb chops are seared, they will bake for a short time at 375°F.

2-5 minutes for medium-rare to medium, or
5-8 minutes for medium-well to well done.

Let rest for at least 5 minutes.

THE TRADITIONAL CHESAPEAKE BAY BAKED ROCKFISH STUFFED WITH CRAB IMPERIAL

HOME CHEF
Dr. Carolyn Tabb

INGREDIENTS

1 lb. of Maryland jumbo lump crabmeat
4 wild striped bass fillets, about 5 oz. each
1 egg yolk
¾ cup of mayonnaise
1 tsp of Old Bay seasoning
1 tbsp of yellow French's mustard
1 tbsp of Coleman's mustard
½ tsp of Worcestershire sauce
2 tsp of whole milk
1 tsp of Italia's lemon juice
1 tbsp of fresh parsley
Salt to taste

DIRECTIONS

1. Preheat oven to 350°F.
2. Empty jumbo lump crab meat into a bowl and clean out any additional shells.
3. In a small bowl, whip the egg and Old Bay together until doubled in volume. Fold in mayonnaise, mustard, and Worcestershire sauce into the mixture thoroughly.
4. Reserve 25% of the mixture and add milk, lemon, and parsley to that reserved amount; this will serve as the final glaze.
5. Pour the remaining sauce over the crab to create the imperial stuffing. Season with a pinch of salt.
6. Lightly fold the ingredients together, making sure not to break the crab lumps. Lightly rinse each filet in cold salted water, then pat dry. Season each filet with salt.
7. Create an oval-shaped hole with each filet and stuff the imperial stuffing into the oval.
8. Evenly coat each stuffed rockfish filet with the reserved imperial sauce.
9. Bake for 10-14 minutes, until the center of the fish and crab imperial stuffing are hot. The internal temperature should be 140 degrees. The glaze should be lightly browned and slightly puffed.

BUTTERY SAUTEED GREEN BEANS

HOME CHEF
Dr. Carolyn Tabb

DIRECTIONS

1. In a large skillet, heat the butter over medium-high heat.
2. When the butter stops foaming, add the green beans, and sea salt.
3. Cook, stirring often, about 5 minutes.
4. Add ground black pepper, garlic, and crushed red peppers.
5. Continue to cook, stirring often, for about 5 more minutes, until the beans are tender but not mushy.

INGREDIENTS

2 tbsp unsalted butter

½ lb green beans and ½ lb wax yellow beans ends trimmed

½ tsp sea salt

½ tsp ground black pepper

1 tbsp minced fresh garlic, if desired

¼ tsp crushed red pepper

SEAFOOD LASAGNA

HOME CHEF

Dr. Carolyn Tabb

INGREDIENTS

1 lb. of lasagna noodles
Sea salt to taste
2 tbsp of extra-virgin olive oil
1 lb. large shrimp, peeled, deveined, tails removed, and steamed
Fresh ground black pepper
Juice of ½ lemon
2 garlic cloves, minced
6 tbsp of butter

ALFREDO SAUCE
½ cup of heavy cream
1 cup of evaporated milk
½ cup whole milk
½ cup freshly grated Parmesan and Romano cheeses mixed together

5 cups of freshly grated Mozzarella cheese
2 tbsp of fresh chopped parsley, add more for garnish
16 oz. of ricotta cheese
2 large eggs, lightly beaten
1 lb. lump crab meat, deshelled
1 large finely diced onion
1 tbsp Italian seasoning
1 package of frozen chopped broccoli florets, thawed and drained
1 package of frozen chopped spinach, thawed, and drained

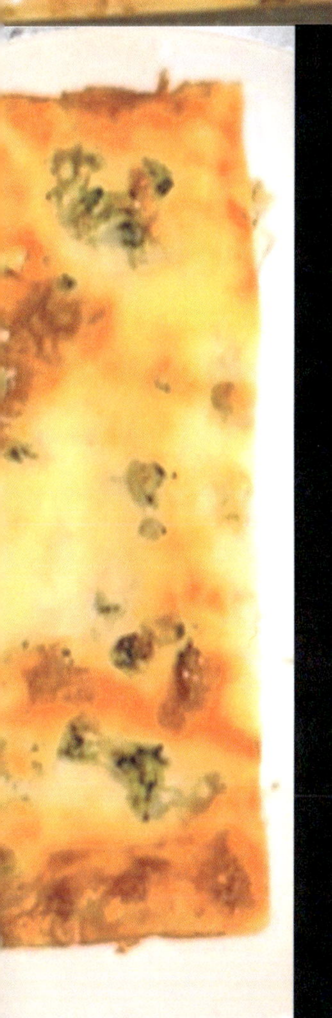

DIRECTIONS

In a small bowl, combine crab and steamed shrimp, then set aside. In another bowl, combine ricotta cheese, eggs, and Italian seasoning until smooth, then set aside.

In a large skillet, sauté onion and garlic in butter until tender. Gradually add whole milk and evaporated milk. Bring to a boil; cook and stir for 2 minutes or until thickened. Reduce heat; stir in Parmesan cheese, sea salt, and ground black pepper until cheese is melted.

Coat a greased, shallow 4 qt. baking dish with a layer of ricotta cheese. Layer with three noodles, spinach, and broccoli. Top with 1/3 of the ricotta mixture, 1/3 of the mozzarella cheese, and 1/3 of the Alfredo sauce.

Layer three noodles on top with crab and shrimp mixture. Repeat with ricotta mixture, mozzarella cheese, and Alfredo sauce. Layer with remaining noodles, spinach, and broccoli. Repeat with the remaining ricotta mixture, mozzarella, and Alfredo sauce. Sprinkle with the remaining Parmesan/Romano cheese blend and mozzarella cheese.

Bake uncovered at 350°F for 45-55 minutes, or until you have a 160°F thermometer reading.

Let stand for 10 minutes before cutting.

GLADYS' 123 CAKE

HOME CHEF

Dr. Carolyn Tabb

DIRECTIONS

Do not preheat the oven.

Grease and flour the bottom, sides, and center tube of a 9-inch tube cake pan.

In a large bowl, cream the butter and sugar together until smooth and fluffy. Add the eggs one at a time, mixing well after each addition. Be careful not to overbeat.

With the mixer on low speed, add the flour and cream alternately, beginning and ending with the flour. Mix until just combined. Stir in the vanilla extract.

Pour the batter evenly into the prepared pan. Place the cake into a cold oven. Set the oven temperature to 325°F and begin timing immediately. Bake for 1 hour and 15 minutes, or until a toothpick inserted into the center comes out clean.

Allow the cake to cool in the pan for 30 minutes, then carefully turn it out onto a wire rack to cool completely.

INGREDIENTS

1 cup (2 sticks) of salted butter, room temperature
3 cups of sugar
6 large eggs. room temperature
3 cups of King Arthur's cake flour. sifted
1 can of evaporated milk
1 tsp of Island Spice vanilla extract